Marine Rose

Sophia de Mello Breyner

Marine Rose

Selected Poems

translated by Ruth Fainlight

BLACK SWAN BOOKS

PQ
9261
A6893
A24
1986

First English translation

Published by

BLACK SWAN BOOKS Ltd.
P. O. Box 327
Redding Ridge, CT 06876
U.S.A.

ISBN 0-933806-37-X

LC Card: 86-17168

CONTENTS

FOREWORD

SOPHIA DE MELLO BREYNER writes from a world of white beaches and glittering light reflecting from both the Atlantic Ocean that washes the shores of Portugal and the sea surrounding the Greek islands. Portugal and Greece—the open Atlantic, the closed Aegean: the two geographic extremes of Europe. Unified by the light and the sea wind, territory of birds, trees, and the moon—it is a world inhabited more by elements and angels and gods than by humans.

The profound and liberating effect of Greece, its physical actuality—a world of gods and presences—one of the primal roots of European culture, has helped give birth to some of the author's finest work. The Greek world, the past glories of the Portuguese navigators, the life and work of the great twentieth century Portuguese poet Fernando Pessoa—all resonate throughout her poetry.

These poems have been selected from nine of the books Sophia de Mello Breyner has published since 1944 to the present and include as well some of her latest work (with first publication here of "Princess of the Extreme City").

In working on the translation into English of these poems, I have had the assistance of the author herself and am duly thankful for her intimate involvement in the project. These translations would not have been possible without the inestimable help of Suzette Macedo. For my initial acquaintance with the poet's work, I am profoundly grateful to Helder Macedo—as well as for his careful reading of these renditions and his always helpful comments.

— Ruth Fainlight

Mid-Day

MID-DAY. No one in this corner of the beach.
The sun on high, deep, enormous, open
Has cleared the sky of every god.
Implacable as punishment, light falls.
There are no ghosts, nor souls,
And the huge, solitary, ancient ocean
Seems to applaud.

Apollo Musagetes

YOU WERE the first day, entire and pure
Bathing horizons with glory.

You were the spirit that spoke from everywhere
You were the burgeoning dawn
In the sea air.
You were a sail drinking space-winds
You were the luminous gesture of two arms
Open, limitless.
You were the sea's innocence and force
Through you I learned love's wisdom.

Dream and presence
Of a life in flower
Mastered and delayed.

You were the supreme measure, the eternal canon
Upright, pure, perfect and ordered
In the heart of life and further than life
In the heart of secret rhythms.

White House

WHITE HOUSE facing an enormous sea
With your sand garden and sea flowers
And your unbroached silence where the miracle
Of everything I had is still asleep.

I shall come back to you after the doubtful
Warmth of all those given gestures
When the tumult and desert are past
The ghosts kissed, and the murmurs
Of the uncertain earth have been traversed.

There, reborn into my own world
Redemption will come through your limits
Where not one thing has been lost
The miracle of everything I had.

Who Are You

WHO ARE YOU who hurry forward with the night
Treading white moonlight into the paths
Under the murmur of inspired leaves?

Perfection is born from the echo of your steps
And your presence awakens the richness
To which things have been destined.

The story of the night is the gesture of your arms
The eagerness of wind your youth
And your wanderings the beauty of highways.

Never Again

Never again
Will you walk those simple paths.

Never again be able to feel
Invulnerable and actual.
Lost forever,
What you sought above all else:
The richness of every presence.

And always the same dream, the same absence.

What More of Myself Can I Uproot

WHAT MORE of myself can I uproot
To help me bear the gift of your touch?
Red angel of wind and solitude
Who showed me the sea, and space, and god.

That last row of houses against the sky
Already is huge, winged, weightless and blue.
No gesture, no destiny is brief
Because in all are restless wings.

Later, sunset burns the houses,
Sky and fire penetrate the earth,
And black night comes pulsing like coals
In an endless crescendo to exile us.

I Feel the Dead

I FEEL the dead in the cold of violets
And that great vagueness in the moon.

The earth is doomed to be a ghost,
She who rocks all death in herself.

I know I sing at the edge of silence,
I know I dance around suspension,
Possess around dispossession.

I know I pass around the mute dead
And hold within myself my own death.

But I have lost my being in so many beings,
Died my life so many times,
Kissed my ghosts so many times,
Known nothing of my acts so many times,
That death will be simply like going
From inside the house into the street.

One Day

ONE DAY dead tired worn out we shall
Go back and live as plainly as animals
Even so tired again we shall flourish
Living brothers of the sea and the pinewoods.

The wind will blow away our weariness
The thousand unreal anxious gestures
And our slack limbs surely will regain
The weightless speed of animals.

Only then shall we be able to move
Through the mystery nurtured and lulled
By green pinewoods and the sea's voice
And let its words grow in us.

The Angel

THE ANGEL who hovers about me and spies on me,
And cruelly fights me, that day
Came to sit by the side of my bed
And lulled me to sleep, singing in his breast.

He who will indifferently watch and hear me
Suffer, or with me ferociously struggle,
He who gave me over to loneliness,
Placed his hand on my hand.

And it was as if everything were blotted out,
As if the whole world quietened,
And my freed being at last flowered,
And I was lulled in perfect silence.

Across Countries

ACROSS COUNTRIES and landscapes
They go to find the images
Embraced by earth's warm limbs
Of flesh and foliage.

Light was the light of their hair,
Wind, the wind through their fingers.
Their bodies pursued a thousand secrets
And had the balance of forests.

And freed, they leave again
Between sunset's black bonfires.

And there: the rhythmic heart of a god
Forsaken and alone before the heavens.

Tristan and Isolde

OVER the September sea veiled with mist
The veiled sun sinks
Impregnating with gold the foam
Where the vastest adventure blows.

Tristan and Isolde whom forever I saw passing
Along furthest maritime horizons
Pierced like the sea
By rhythms' fantastic fatality
Move in this afternoon's agony
Where a sister-yearning to theirs burns.

Tristan and Isolde who like the Autumn
Revolve from abandonment to abandon,
Bearing unsayable within themselves
The ecstatic presence of death.

Eurydice

NIGHT is the mantle she drags
Over the sad dust of my essence
When I hear her dying chant
In which all my heart perishes.

Wide across the sky her flying hair
From each palm ocean's voices echo
Crowned with stars and smiling
She passes through the zone of nightmare.

She came like someone who does not exist
Told me of everything mortal
And slowly, unmade herself back into air
Sad to be ghostly, flowing water.

There Are Gardens

THERE ARE gardens invaded by moonlight
That vibrate in the silence like lyres.
Hold your love safe between your fingers
In this April garden where you breathe.

Life will not come—your hands
Cannot pluck from others the sweetness
Of flowers swaying in the wind.

If only your body were made of moonlight,
If only you were a garden full of pools,
The trees blossoming, the profusion
Of their black shadow along the paths.

After Gulping the Moonlight

AFTER gulping the moonlight, drunk on horizons,
We knew that living meant to embrace
The murmur of pinewoods, blueness of mountains,
All the sea's green gardens.

But we are lonely visitants,
Not for us the fruit or flowers,
Appearances of sea and sky
Fade into dream-phantoms.

Why gardens we cannot harvest
At the birth of limpid dawns, why
Sea and sky if we shall never be
Gods enough to live there?

I Called

I CALLED myself when the sea sang
I called myself when the fountains ran
I called myself when the heroes died
And every being gave a sign to me.

My hands support the stars,
I hold my soul secure so that the melody
That goes from flower to flower will not be broken,
Pull sea apart from sea to take into myself
And my heart's beat sustains the rhythm of things.

Day of Sea

DAY OF SEA in the sky, made
From shadows and horses and plumes.

Day of sea in my room—cube
Where my sleepwalker's movements slide
Between animal and flower, like medusas.

Day of sea in the sea, high day
Where my gestures are seagulls who lose themselves
Spiralling over the clouds, over the spume.

Passing Cars

PASSING CARS make the house shudder
The house where only I am.
Already things have lived themselves out:
In the air pockets of dead space
Shapes etched in the vacuum
Of voices and gestures which long ago existed.
And my hands retain nothing.

Yet still I scrutinize the night
And stand in need of every leaf.

Revolve and gyrate your life in the air
Far from me here—
Truly to plumb this torment of nothingness
I need solitude.

Rather this wilderness of eternal partings
Plans and questions,
Of mortal combat with the burning
Weight of deaths and griefs
Rather solitude because it is perfect.

I affirm my life's nakedness.
Each chance event dispensable.

I only claim the sense of everything stopped
With eternity floating over the mountains.

Garden, unregainable garden
Our limbs encircling your absence.
Leaves whisper your secret one to the other,
And my love is as covert as fear.

Sibyls

Sibyls of deep caves, of petrifaction,
Totally loveless and sightless,
Feeding nothingness as if a sacred fire
While shadow unmakes night and day
Into the same light of fleshless horror.

Drive out that foul dew
Of impacted nights, the sweat
Of forces turned against themselves
When words batter the walls
In blind, wild swoops of trapped birds
And the horror of being winged
Shrills like a clock through a vacuum.

Listen

LISTEN:
Everything is calm and smooth and sleeping.
The walls apparent, the floor reflecting,
And painted on the glass of the window,
The sky, green emptiness, two trees.
Close your eyes and rest no less profoundly
Than any other thing which never flowered.

Don't touch anything, don't look, don't recollect.
One step enough
To shatter the furniture baked
By endless, unused days of sunlight.

Don't remember, don't anticipate.
You do not share the nature of a fruit:
Nothing here that time or sun will ripen.

I Call You

I CALL You because it's all just beginning
And time is lengthened most by endurance.

I ask You to set me free,
One look to cleanse and finish me.

So many things I do not want to see.

I beg You to manifest.
Ask You to flood everything.
Your kingdom to anticipate
And inundate the earth
In rash, ferocious Spring.

The Birds

HEAR what strange night birds
I have outside my window:
Birds with shrill wild cries,
Breast the colour of dawn, beak purple
They talk to each other of night, draw
From the abyss of slow still night
Cruel and strident words.
They thrust their claws into the moonlight
And the breath of terror falls
From their heavy wings.

You Sleep Cradled

YOU SLEEP cradled by rocks
And the wind comes and gibbers in my ear.
I listen, seek, call out but you don't answer,
And the world returned to shadow.

I also am trapped, encased, a prisoner
Who would like to break through into daylight,
To resurrect, breathe deep, to see again,
But all the world returned to shadow.

And the ocean's voice weighed down the land
        and sky
A voice which is laden, which falters
And never stops.

White birds violate the windows,
Anemones scintillate upon the rocks:
The terror of my loneliness, of listening
With this dead moment caught between my fingers.

A White Day

GIVE ME a white day, a sea of belladonna,
One movement
Integral, united, and lulled
Into a single moment.

I want to walk like one asleep
Between nameless floating countries.

Images so mute
Looking at them it seems
My eyes are shut.

One day when not to know might have been possible.

Beach

THE PINES moan when the wind passes
The sun beats on the earth and the stones burn.

Fantastic sea gods stroll at the edge of the world
Crusted with salt and brilliant as fishes.

Sudden wild birds hurled
Against the light into the sky like stones
Mount and die vertically
Their bodies taken by space.

The waves butt as if to smash the light
Their brows ornate with columns.

And an ancient nostalgia of being a mast
Sways in the pines.

The Boats

FISHERMEN'S BOATS sleep on the beach
Motionless but opening
Their statue's eyes

And the curve of their beaks
Pecks at solitude.

Coral

HE WENT and came
And asked each thing
Its name.

———

"Coral" is the name of a cat.

Poetry

OH POETRY—how much from you I've asked!
I live here in no-man's land
And don't know who I am—I who did not die
When the king was killed and the kingdom divided.

Penelope

DURING THE NIGHT I unweave my path,
What I am weaving is not truth,
But time, to fill the dead time,
And each day I move away and every night
    come nearer.

Black Trees That Whisper

BLACK TREES that whisper in my ear,
Leaves that do not sleep, swollen with fever,
What goodbye is this dismissing me
And this endless plea that the wind launches
And this imploring voice, imploring forever
With no-one ever to give an answer?

Torpid Shores

TORPID SHORES open their arms,
And a great ship departs in silence.
Gulls fly at high perpendicular angles,
The light is born, and death is perfect.

A great ship departs, abandoning
The white columns of a vacant harbor.
And its own face seeks itself emerging
From the headless torso of the city.

A great ship unloosed departs
Sculpting head-on the north wind.
Perfect the ocean's blue, death perfect—
Awesome clear sharp forms.

Poem From a Book Destroyed

How STRANGE it is, my freedom
Things let me pass,
Open aisles of emptiness so I can pass
How strange to live without food
Nothing inside us that wants or wastes
How strange it is, not to know

In the Divided Time

AND NOW, Gods, what shall I say of myself?
Torpid afternoons expire in the garden.
I've forgotten about you and without memory
I keep to the paths where time, like a monster,
Daily devours more of its own flesh.

Sonnet to Eurydice

Lost Eurydice who in the odors
And voices of ocean is seeking Orpheus
Absence that peoples land and sky
And muffles the whole world with silence

Thus I gulped the mists of morning
And renounced life and identity
In search of a face that was mine
My own face, secret and authentic

But neither in tides nor illusions
Did I find you. Only the smooth pure face
Of the landscape rose before me

And slowly I became transparent
A dead woman born into your likeness
And lost in this world, and barren

Cante Jondo

ON A NIGHT without moon my love died
Nameless men carried through the street
A dead and naked body that was mine.

Biography

I HAD FRIENDS who died, others who left
Others broke their face against time.
I hated what was easy
I sought myself in the sea the wind the light.

I Will Not Offend You

I WILL NOT offend you with poems

My eyes close when I think of you
I will not make a song from my remorse

With trees and skies but not poems
Too human to be able to express
Your world was simple and difficult
Ordinary and limpid

The Three Fates

THE THREE Fates who spin the wrong
Ways where laughing we betray
That pure time we never get near enough
The Fates make sure we have bad luck.

They wait for us on false paths
Where blind we sell ourselves short for someone
We do not want to be or love
Who holds us captive and constrained.

And never again the pure blowing wind
Will take us to the longed-for world
Never again the mysterious face

Be conquered and become our face
Nor the gods grant us that state
Invented for our expectations.

This Is the Time

THIS IS the time
Of a jungle without meaning

Even the blue air coagulates to gratings
And the sun's light becomes obscene.

This is the night
Thick with jackals
Weighted with grief

The time when men give up.

Body

BODY serenely built
For a life that afterwards wrecks itself
In rage and disappointment turned
Against the total pureness of your shoulders.

If only I could hold you in the mirror
Absent and mute to all other companions
Keep the bright knot of your knees
That shatter through the glass of mirrors.

If only I could keep you in those afternoons
That drew the line of your flanks
The grateful air enclosed.

Brilliant body of vivid nudity
Built by recurring waves
Into a temple resting on its columns.

Because

BECAUSE OTHERS wear masks but you do not
Because others use virtue
To buy what cannot be pardoned.
Because others are frightened but you are not.

Because the others are whited sepulchres
Where corruption sprouts in silence.
Because the others are silenced but you are not.

Because others can be bought and sold
And their gestures always pay dividends.
Because others are cunning but you are not.

Because others take cover in the shadows
And you walk hand in hand with danger.
Because others calculate but you do not.

Muse

MUSE teach me the song
Revered and primordial
The song for everyone
Believed by all

Muse teach me the song
The true brother of each thing
Incendiary of the night
And evening's secret

Muse teach me the song
That takes me home
Without delay or haste
Changed to plant or stone

Or changed into the wall
Of the first house
Or become the murmur
Of sea all around

(I remember the floor
Of well-scrubbed planks
Its soapy smell
Keeps coming back)

Muse teach me the song
Of the sea's breath
Heaving with brilliants
Muse teach me the song
Of the white room
And the square window

So I can say
How evening there
Touched door and table
Cup and mirror
How it embraced

Because time pierces
Time divides
And time thwarts
Tears me alive
From the walls and floor
Of the first house

Muse teach me the song
Revered and primordial
To fix the brilliance
Of the polished morning

That rested its fingers
Gently on the dunes
And whitewashed the walls
Of those simple rooms

Muse teach me the song
That chokes my throat

Morning

LIKE A FRUIT that being
Opened proves
The freshness at its centre

So is this morning
Into which I enter

The Conquest of Cacela

THE STRONGHOLDS were conquered
To subdue their power, the seaports
Besieged for their treasure

But they wanted Cacela
Only because of its beauty

In the Poem

To BRING the picture the wall the wind
The flower the glass the shine on wood
And the cold chaste clearness of water
To the clean severe world of the poem

To save from death decay and ruin
The actual moment of vision and surprise
And keep in the real world
The real gesture of a hand touching the table.

Behold Me

BEHOLD me
Having shed all my cloaks
Turned away from seers magicians and gods
To stand alone before silence
The silence and splendor of your face.

But of all those absent you are the most absent
Neither your arm supports nor your hands touch me
My heart descends time's steps where you are not
And to meet you
Is empty space and plains of silence

The night is dark
Dark and transparent
But your face is beyond the opacity of time
And I do not live in the gardens of your silence
Because of all the absent you are the most absent.

With You to Cross the World's Desert

WITH YOU to cross the world's desert
Together face death's terror
To see the truth to lose fear
I followed in your steps.

For you I left my realm my secret
My swift night my silence
My round pearl and its orient
My mirror, life and image
Abandoned the gardens of paradise.

Out here in the unveiled light of hard day
Without mirrors I saw that I was naked
And the wilderness was called time.

And so you dressed me with your gestures
And I learned to live in the full wind.

City

THE ALMOST-VISIBLE threats mount.
From the exhausted horizon
Dead moons are born.
And I am strangled by great tentacles
In the sadness of streets.

Sounion

LIGHT'S NAKEDNESS (in which outside is inside)
Wind's nakedness (surrounding itself)
The nakedness of sea (duplicated by salt)

The Flute

In the room's corner the shadow played
    its little flute
It was then I remembered the cisterns
    and sea-nettles
And the mortal glitter of the naked beach

Night's ring was solemnly placed on my finger
And the silent fleet continued its immemorial journey

Sensitive People

SENSITIVE PEOPLE are not able
To kill chickens
Yet they are able
To eat chickens

Money smells of a pauper and smells
Of the clothes of his body
Those clothes
That after the rain dried on his body
Because there were no others
Money smells of poverty and smells
Of clothes
That after sweating were not washed
Because there were no others

"You will earn your bread by the sweat of your brow"
So on us it was imposed
And not:
"By the sweat of others you will earn your bread."

The temple money-changers
The builders
Of grand overblown heavy statues
O ye, full of devotion and profit

Forgive them Lord
Because they do know what they do.

March

ON THE DESERT MARCH I knew
That some would die

But I thought under the round sky
—Where
Is the limit of my love and my strength?

And it was I who died before the next oasis
With my throat dry and the boundless weight
Of the sun on my shoulders

It was I who died blinded with whiteness
Too tired to see mirages

I knew
That someone
Before the next oasis was going to die.

Twilight of the Gods

A SMILE of amazement appeared in the Aegean islands
And Homer made royal-purple flower on the sea
The Kouros moved forward exactly one step
Athena's paleness glittered in the daylight

In that time the gods' clarity conquered the monsters
    on all the temple-pediments
And the Persians retreated to their empire's
    furthest limits

We celebrated the victory: darkness
Was exposed and sacrificed in great white courtyards
The hoarse cry of the chorus purified the city

Swift joy circled the ships
Like dolphins
Our body was naked because it had found
Its exact measure
We invented: the light inherent to Sounion's columns
Each day the world became more ours

But then they were extinguished
The ancient gods, internal sun of things
Then there opened the void which separates us
    from things
We are hallucinated by absence, drunk with absence
And to Julian's heralds, the Sibyl replied:

"Go tell the king that the beautiful palace lies broken
    on the ground
Phoebus now has no house nor prophetic bay-tree
    nor melodious fountain
The talking water is silent"

Winter Poetry

I

WINTER POETRY: poetry of a godless time
Choosing
Carefully between the remnants

Poetry of shamefaced words
Poetry of the scruples of words

Poetry of repentant words
That dare to say:

Silk   nacre   rose

Tree abstract and unleaved
In the winter of our discontent

II

Aseptic pincers
Placing the word-thing
On the line of the paper
On the library shelf

III

That dare to say:

Silk   nacre   rose

For no one has woven the silk with his own hands
   —during long
days on long spindles and with fine silky fingers

And no one has garnered from the margin of morning
   the rose-light
and heavy face of sweetness

For the river has ceased to be sacred
   and thus is not even a river
And the universe does not blossom
   from the hand of a god
from the gesture and breath of a joyful god
   and from the vehemence of a god

And man, brooding on the margin of his fate,
   tries to obtain a permit
to live in the survivors' make-shift barracks

IV

My heart seeks the words of summer
Seeks the promised summer of words

On Transparency

LORD, free us from the dangerous game of
    transparency
There are no corals or shells in the depths
    of our soul's sea
But a suffocated dream
And we do not know exactly what dreams are
Silent conductors muffled song
That one day suddenly emerge
In the great smooth courtyard of disasters

The Small Square

MY LIFE had taken the form of a small square
That autumn when your death was being
    meticulously organized
I clung to the square because you loved
The humble and nostalgic humanity of small shops
Where shopkeepers fold and unfold ribbons and cloth
I tried to become you because you were going to die
And all my life there would cease to be mine
I tried to smile as you smiled
At the newspaper seller at the tobacco seller
At the woman without legs who sold violets
I asked the woman without legs to pray for you
I lit candles at all the altars
Of the churches standing in the corner of that square
Hardly had I opened my eyes when I saw and read
The vocation for eternity written on your face
I summoned up the streets places people
Who were the witnesses of your face
So they would call you so they would unweave
The tissue that death was binding around you

In Crete

IN Crete
Where the Minotaur rules
I bathed in the sea

There is a rapid dance danced before a bull
In the day's most ancient youth

No drug altered sheltered or concealed me
I only drank retsina having poured on the earth
    that part which belongs to the gods

Crete's flowers
I decked myself with and chewed the living bitterness
    of herbs
So that fully awake I could commune with the land
Crete's earth
I kissed like Odysseus
I walked in the naked light

I myself was devastated like a city in ruins
Which no one rebuilt
But in the sun of my empty courtyards
Fury reigns intact
And with me penetrates the sea's depths
Because I belong to the race of those
    who dive with open eyes
And recognize the abyss stone by stone
    anemone by anemone, flower by flower
And the sea of Crete is all blue inside
Incredible offering of primordial joy
Where the somber Minotaur navigates

Paintings waves columns and planes—
In Crete
Fully awake I moved across the day
And walked inside strident and scarlet palaces
Hoarse successive palaces
Where the breathing of the murmured darkness rises
And eyes half blue with shadow and terror fix us
Fast to the day—
I walked through the dual palace of combat
    and confrontation
Where the Prince of Lilies lifts his arms to the
    morning

No drug altered sheltered or concealed me
The Dionysus who dances with me in the waves
    is not sold in any black market
But grows like the flower of those whose being
Endlessly seeks and loses itself is disunited
    and reunited
And this is the dance of being

In Crete
The brick walls of the Minoan city
Are made of mud kneaded with seaweed
And when I turned back to my shadow
I saw the sun was blue that touched my shoulder

In Crete where the Minotaur rules
    I moved across the wave
Open eyed fully awake
Without drugs and without a philtre
Only wine drunk confronting the solemnity of
    things—
Because I belong to the race of those who journey
    through the labyrinth
Without ever losing the flaxen thread of the word

Cyclades

(invoking Fernando Pessoa)

THE FRONTAL CLARITY of this place imposes
   your presence
Your name emerges as if the negative
Of what you were develops here

You lived in reverse
Incessant traveller of the inverse
Exempt from yourself
Widower of yourself
Lisbon your stage-set
You were the tenant of a rented room above a dairy
Competent clerk in a business firm
Ironic delicate polite frequenter of the Old Town bars
Judicious visionary of cafés facing the Tagus

(Where still in the marble-topped tables
We seek the cold trace of your hands
—Their imperceptible fingering)

Dismembered by the furies of that non-life
Marginal to yourself to others and to life
You kept all your notebooks up to date
With meticulous exactitude drew the maps
Of the multiple navigations of your absence—

What never was and what you never were stays said
Like an island rising up windward
With plumb-line compass astrolabe and sounding-lead
You determined the measure of exile

You were born later
Others had found the truth
The sea-route to India already was discovered
Nothing was left of the gods
But their uncertain passage
Through the murmur and smell of those landscapes
And you had many faces
So that being no one you could say everything
You travelled the reverse the inverse the adverse

And yet obstinately I invoke—O divided one—
The instant that might unite you
And celebrate your arrival at the islands
    you never reached

These are the archipelagos that float
    across your face
The swift dolphins of joy
The gods did not grant nor you wanted

This is the place where the flesh of statues
    like trembling willows
Pierced by light's breathing
Shines with matter's blue breath
On beaches where mirrors turn towards the sea

Here the enigma that always puzzled me
Is more naked and vehement therefore I implore:

"Why were your movements broken
Who encircled you by walls and chasms
Who spilt your secrets onto the ground?"

Invoke you as though you arrived in this boat
And it were your feet stepping onto the islands
Whose excessive overwhelming nearness
Was like a loved face bending too close

In the summer of this place I call you
Who hibernated your life like an animal
        through the harsh season
Who needed to be distant like someone standing back
        to see the picture better
And willed the distance he suffered

I call you—I gather the pieces the ruins the
        fragments—
Because the world cracked like a quarry
And capitals and arms columns shattered to splinters
Heave from the ground
And only a scattering of potsherds is left
        of the amphora
Before which the gods become foreigners

Yet here the wheat-colored goddesses
Raise the long harp of their fingers
To charm the blue sun where I invoke you
And invoke the impersonal word of your absence

If only this festive moment could break your
        mourning
O self-elected widower
And if being and to be would coincide
In the one marriage

As if your boat were waiting in Thasos
As if Penelope
In her high chamber
Were weaving you into her hair

25th April 1974

THIS is the dawn I was waiting for
The first day whole and pure
When we emerged from night and silence
Alive into the substance of time

NAVIGATIONS

"Navigations" is comprised of three poems: "Lisbon," "The Islands," and "Drift."

Lisbon

I SAY:
"Lisbon"
When I cross the river—coming from the south—
And the city I approach opens as though born
    from its name
Opens and surges into its night-time spaces
Into its long shining of blue and river
Its body of shaped hills—
I see it better because I speak
It all shows better because I speak
Exposes better its being and need
Because I say
Lisbon, that name of being and non-being
With its secret meanders of amazement, insomnia,
    and tin shacks
And secret glitter of something theatrical
Its conniving smile of intrigue and masks
While the wide ocean dilates west
Lisbon rocking like a great boat
Lisbon cruelly built along its own absence
I say the city's name
I say it in order to see

The Islands

I

WE NAVIGATED East—
The long coast
Was a dense somnolent green

A motionless green under an absent wind
As far as the white shore color of roses
Touched by transparent waters

Then appeared the luminous islands
Of a blue so pure and violent
Surpassing the brilliance of heavens
Navigated by miraculous herons

And memory and time were quenched

II

Abstract navigation
Intent as a fish the plane follows the route
Seen from above the earth becomes a map

But suddenly
We cross into the Orient through the great gate
Of blue sapphires in the glinting sea

III

The light of dawn's appearance
Shone in the hollow of wandering
Sails testing the distances

Here they let down the dark anchors
Those who went seeking
The real face of the visible
And dared—most fantastic adventure—
To live the whole of the possible

IV

dolce color d'oriental zaffiro
—Dante

Here they sighted islands rise like flowers
Those who came by sea heading south
And rounded the cape to face the dawn sky
Steering the thrust of the black keels

And under tall clouds like white lyres
Their eyes truly saw
The sweet blue of the East and of sapphires

V

We saw the visible in all its vehemence
The total exposure of appearance
And what we had not dared to dream
Was real

VI

They navigated from the chart they had to make

(Leaving behind the plots and conversations
Muffled intrigues of brothel and palace)

The wise men had already concluded
That only the known could exist:
Ahead lay only the unnavigable
Below the sun's clamor, the uninhabitable

Undeciphered the writing of those other stars
In the silence of cloudy zones
The shivering compass needle touching space

Then appeared the luminous coasts
Silences the palm-groves' ardent coolness
And the brilliance of the visible face to face

VII

Difficult to face your death head-on
And never expect you again in the mirrors of fog

Drift

I

SMOOTHED SILENCE under the trade-winds
—The sails all gently swollen—
A shine like fish scales on the high seas
And to larboard the newly-sighted coasts
Below the clamor of ecstatic moonlight
A motionless silence of palm-groves

II

It was the Route of Gold
But on the high seas
Or beaches of swaying palm-groves
Surprise guided us—
Water slid down all the images

III

Nude they plunged from smooth wide shores
Others lost themselves in the sudden blueness of
   storms

IV

But he rounded the Cape and did not find India
And the sea devoured him with its instinct for destiny

V

I'll tell about black naked men
And how because none of us could
Comprehend one word they said
We danced together to be understood

VI

I'll tell you of a long white strand
And naked black men who danced
To hold up the sky with their lances

VII

Others report, Sire, the courses and sailings
I will tell you of the glistening shore
Of creation's first morning

I will tell of innocent nakedness
The coy sweetness bright swiftness
Of men still the color of clay who believed
We were their old paternal gods
Come back again

VIII

I saw waters capes and islands
The rocking line of palms
I saw lagoons as blue as sapphires
Darting birds and furtive animals
I saw prodigies horrors marvels
I saw naked men dancing on the beaches
And I heard the deep sound of their words
Which none of us could understand
I saw spears and arrows and lances
Gold on the surface of crisp waves
And the varied dazzle of other metals
I saw pearls and shells and corals
Deserts fountains shimmering plains
I saw Eurydice's face in the fog
The freshness of everything natural
But no sign of Prester John

The orders I took were not fulfilled
And telling all I saw, still
Don't know what I discovered, what I missed

IX

Cities and ambuscades
But also
The amazement of such grand architecture
The silks the perfumes the sweetness
Of voices and gestures

The great courtyards of night and their flower
Of panic and stillness

X

Shadowy gods
Terror's ancient lords
Breath like statues hovering
In the restless light of altar lamps

XI

Wide eyes of the navigator
Here light shade and color change
And faces and gestures modulate
Forming strange elaborations
Wave and rock have another outline
The boats are followed by dragon's tails

XII

Cupidity gnawing the green surprise of islands to
    windward
Cupidity gnawing the bare face of discovery

XIII

The faintest humming
In the hushed silence
Of night's stillness

Like someone unable
To find his own image

XIV

Athwart your heart a ship passed
And still follows its course without you

XV

Inverse navigation
Tedium without the Tagus
The hostile grayness of rooms
Desolate streets
(Line by line I have returned)
Verso to reverse
Lisbon anti-country of life

XVI

The king of Cyprus
Has a certain mystery
Not only because he's Greek
Being somewhat Assyrian
But a peculiar quietude
A certain withdrawal
Between two wars—
His body a stalk of corn
A column of truce
Inhabiting a certain pause
The like of which I never found
—The clarity of islands
However much I sought

XVII

Manueline style:
Not the Roman nave ordering
Sown seed out from the earth
Nor the thrusting corn stalk
Of the Greek column
But the flower of chance whose odyssey
Aggregates origins

The Minotaur

THUS THE MINOTAUR for so long latent
Suddenly leaps into our life
With the raw vehemence of a beast unsated

The King of Ithaca

THIS CIVILIZATION of ours is so wrong that
In it thought is divorced from the hand

Ulysses king of Ithaca worked the wood for his boat
And boasted also that he knew how to drive
A straight furrow across the field with his plough

Torso

TWISTING HIS TORSO he turned the steamshovel wheel
One September day's decline in the XXth century
On the road that goes from Patras to Athens

His Hellenistic beauty fought the twilight
Muscle masses swollen with effort
Structured the tumult of light and shadow
That wrenches the bodies of lost gods
From the Pergamon friezes

Also in the twilight where I live
The gods are defeated

---

*Author's Note: While the gods are the ostensible victors of the Pergamon
frieze, there is presaged in the monument a subliminal premonition of the
imminent demise of the classical world itself. "Torso" reflects this implied
pathos and expresses a view akin to that of André Malraux in* La Méta-
morphose des Dieux *that the Pergamon frieze depicts "the twilight of
the gods."*

Meditation of the Duke of Gandia
on the Death of Isabel of Portugal

NEVER AGAIN
Will your face be pure, clear, alive
Nor your step like a fugitive wave
Weave itself between the steps of time.
Never again will I give my life to time.

Never again will I serve one who may die.
The slanting light shows me your
Putrescent being. Soon rottenness
Will drink your eyes and your bones
Taking your hand in his hand.

Never again will I love one who cannot live
Forever.
Because I loved as if they were eternal,
The glory, light, and brilliance of your being,
I loved the truth of you and what shone through
And I am left with not even your absence
But these features of disgust and negation
And I close my eyes not to see you.

Never again will I serve one who can die.

The Dead Soldier

THE ENDLESS SKIES gaze at his face
Absolute and sightless
And now the breeze kisses his mouth
That will never kiss anyone else.

His hands still keep the concave shape
of possession, impulse, promise.
And hope slides from his shoulders,
Divided and dispersed by evening.

The light, the hours, the hills
Become a lament around his face
Because he was played and was lost
And across the sky, sudden birds pass.

Writing

IN PALAZZO MOCENIGO where he lived alone
Lord Byron used every grand room
To watch solitude mirror by mirror
And the beauty of doors no one passed through

He heard the marine murmurs of silence
The lost echoes of steps in far corridors
He loved the smooth shine on polished floors
Shadows unrolling under high ceilings
And though he sat in just one chair
Was glad to see the other chairs were empty

Of course no one needs so much space to live
But writing insists on solitudes and deserts
Things to look at as if seeing something else

We can imagine him seated at his table
Imagine the full long throat
The open white shirt
The white paper the spidery writing
And the light of a candle—as in certain paintings—
Focussing all attention

Homage to Ricardo Reis III

THE GODS are absent yet they preside.
　　We inhabit this
　　Ambiguous transparency.

Their thought emerges when everything
　　Suddenly becomes
　　Solemnly exact.

Their gaze guides ours:
　　Our attention to the world
　　Is the observance they claim.

---

*"Ricardo Reis" was one of several pseudonyms ("heteronyms") used by
Fernando Pessoa.*

Homage to Ricardo Reis VI

BROTHER of what I wrote
Now I want distance
Like one who draws back
To see the picture better.
But you, Nera, impose
Laws that are not mine.
Your feet tread the dance
Of measureless shadow
Before the verandah
You scintillate, fugitive
Long hair white wrists
Twisting your tresses
Your taurine face
Erupting from the night
Awakens images
More ancient than the gods.

Princess of the Extreme City
(or The Death of Ritual)

WHEN THE LORD OF SUMMER's palace was invaded
Iso, Princess of the Extreme City
Gravely inclined her small head
In her coral smile teeth gleamed like grains of rice

When they took her collection of jade
A smile creased her fine nostril
Her eyelashes semaphored like butterflies

When they took her red jars illuminated books
Her sandalwood bed
She was pliant and calm
Her eyelashes applauded like black fans
Her lips recited the ancient saying:

He who is dispossessed becomes free

In the lake she saw herself
She was still herself
Pliant and shining as silk
Cool and smooth as jade
Vivid and precious as a painting

Serene as silk she slept that night on a rush mat

But dawn brought a new time to the city

When she awoke
The cortege of hands did not hasten
The hand that places a flower in the vase
The hand that lights the incense
The hand that unrolls the carpet
The hand that makes the harp sing music

The slender firm and subtle hand that paints the eyes'
    contours
The slow cool hand that pours out perfume

No hand invokes the gods' spirit
The roof-guardians
No hand accomplishes the ancient ritual that starts
Day's linear fire
No hand traces the gesture that shapes
Day's celestial form

The walls say:
Stand up alone
You are not an idol you are not divine
Nothing is divine

Like loosened silk sliding to the ground
She swoons

When she returns it is not to her image
All is engulfed and abolished in that sudden vortex

The bamboo's colloquy is silenced
Not even a frog croaks

Like a stalk in the wind her thin neck sways
Her lashes unmoving as those of the blind man who
            for thousands of years near the bridge
                    does not see the river
She trips on her robes like the blind man

Her hands grope the air

High above she hears the sky creak
It is the gods tearing their silken banners of wind

Not to hear the hiss of whetted knives
She plunges to the muddy depths of the lake
Then floats for many days
Centre of a corolla formed
By her wide spreading clothes.

The Art of Poetry

I

IN LAGOS, the sun in August falls straight at sunset, and there are places where the ground itself is whitewashed. The sun is heavy but the light is soft. I am walking along close to the wall but I don't fit into the shadow. The shadow is a narrow ribbon. I dip my hand in it as if I were immersing it in water.

The pottery studio is on a small street across the square, just past the open-air bar and the blacksmith's dark workshop.

I enter the pottery studio. The woman who sells the pieces is small and old, dressed in black. She stands before me, surrounded by pots. To her right and left, the floor and shelves are covered with earthenware, lined up or in heaps and piles: plates, pitchers, jugs and bowls. There are two kinds of clay: pale pink and dark ocher. The clay that men have been learning how to cast on a human scale since time immemorial. Forms that have been passed from hand to hand through the centuries. The pottery studio I'm in could just as well be in Crete. I look at the pale clay pots arrayed in front of me on the floor. Perhaps the art of this period in which I live has taught me to look at them better. Perhaps the art of this period is an ascetic art that has helped us to see more clearly.

The beauty of this pale clay pot is so evident and certain that it cannot be described. But I also know that the word "beauty" is of no consequence. I know that beauty does not exist in and of itself; it is rather the face, the shape or sign of a truth from which it cannot be separated. I am not speaking of aesthetic beauty but of poetic beauty.

I look at the pot: when I fill it with water, it will give me a drink. But it is already giving something to me: peace and contentment, the revelation of being in the world, reconnection.

I look at the pot in the cramped studio. A sweet twilight floats in the air. Outside, the sun. The pot forges an alliance between the sun and me.

I look at the pot, which is identical to the others, a pot countless times reproduced. But no amount of duplication can degrade it, because within it there exists an incorruptible principle.

Outside on the street, under the weight of the same sun, other things, though, are offered to me. Different things. They have nothing in common with me or with the sun. They come from a world where the alliance has been shattered, a world that is not reconnected to either the sun or the moon, to either Isis or Demeter, to either the stars or eternity. A world that may be a habitat but is not a kingdom.

The only kingdom, now, is the one that each person finds and conquers on his own, the alliance that each person forges.

This is the kingdom we search for on the green sea's beaches, in the suspended blue of the night, in the purity of whitewash, in a polished pebble, in the scent of oregano. Like Orpheus' body, which the Furies tore to pieces, this kingdom is in fragments. We attempt to put it back together, to re-establish its unity one piece at a time.

This is why I take the pale clay pot with me, why it is precious to me. I place it on top of the wall, facing the sea. In this place, it is the new image of my alliance with things. This alliance is threatened, this kingdom I passionately discover, reunite, build. This vulnerable kingdom, mortal companion of eternity.

II

POETRY does not require me to specialize because its art is the art of being. Neither does poetry make demands on my time or work. Nor does it ask for knowledge, aesthetics or theory. Instead it requires the completeness of my being, a consciousness that goes deeper than my intelligence, a devotion purer than I can control. It requires unflagging intransigence. It demands that I extract a seamless texture from my life, apart from what shatters, exhausts, pollutes and adulterates. It requires that I live as alert as an antenna, that I be always alive, that I never sleep or forget. It demands unflagging, concentrated, intransigent obstinacy.

Because poetry is my understanding with the world, my intimacy with things, my participation in what is real, my engagement with voices and images. This is why a poem speaks not of ideal life but of actual life: the angle of a window; the reverberation of streets, cities, rooms; shadows along a wall; the appearance of faces; the silence, distance and shine of stars; the breathing of night; the perfume of the linden-flower and oregano.

This relationship with the world defines the poem as poem, as a work of poetic creation. When nothing more is involved than a relationship with matter, skill alone is required.

Skill requires specialization, knowledge, labor, time and an aesthetic. Every poet and every artist is an artisan of language, but the craft of poetry does not come into being on its own, that is, from its relationship with matter. That is the nature of the artisan's art. The craft of poetry is born of the very poetry with which it is consubstantially united. If a poet says "dark," "wide," "white," or "stone," it is because these words name a vision of the world, a connection with things. These words were not chosen on aesthetic grounds, for their beauty: they were chosen for their reality, their necessity, for their poetic ability to forge an alliance. Poetry demands that the poem's "obstinate rigor" be born of un-flagging obstinacy. Each line is as dense and rigid as a bowstring, spoken with precision, because each day is as hard and tense as a bowstring, lived with precision. The internal balance of words is the internal balance of the moments of our life.

In the palpable framework of the poem I see my destination: I recognize my path, my kingdom, my life.

III

MY EARLIEST MEMORY is of a room facing the sea: in it, on top of a table, was a huge red apple. From the shining of the sea and the redness of the apple came an undeniable bliss, naked and complete. There was nothing fantastic or invented about this: I was discovering the very presence of what is real. The works of other artists later confirmed the objectivity of my own vision. I found this same naked, entire bliss, this splendor of the presence of things, in Homer. I found it intensely present, alert and blazing, in the paintings of Amadeo de Sousa-Cardoso. To say that art is a part of culture is somewhat academic and artificial. The work of art is part of what is real: it is destiny, actuality, salvation, and life.

For me, poetry has always been the pursuit of what is real. A poem has always been a circle drawn around something, a circle in which the bird of what is real gets trapped. And if my poetry, which began as air, sea and light, has evolved, it has done so within the scope of this conscientious quest. Because he is motivated by the spirit of truth, whoever searches for the right relationship with a stone, a tree or a river must also search for the right relationship with man. He who sees the frightful splendor of the world is logically led to see the shocking suffering of the world. Whoever observes the phenomenon wants to see the whole thing. It is simply a matter of focus, consistency and discipline.

This is why poetry is also a moral lesson. This is why the very nature of the poet's work leads him to search for justice and why the fight for justice is a basic aspect of all poetic works. In Greek drama we find that the theme of justice is the life-breath of the words. Aeschylus' chorus says: "No wall shall defend him who, drunk with his wealth, pulls down the sacred altar of justice." For justice is inseparable from the balance of things, the order of the world with which the poet wants to integrate his song. It is inseparable from the love which, according to Dante, moves the sun and the stars. It is inseparable from our faith in the world. Just as we passionately rejoice in the splendor of the world, we passionately abhor the suffering of the world. This logic is intimate, private, self-consistent, necessary and trustworthy. The fact that we are made of both praise and protest is witness to the oneness of our conscience.

The poem's moral does not derive from any external code, law or program: because it is a lived reality, it is one with lived time. And in our time, it is necessary for us to raise our level of awareness. After centuries of bourgeois sin, our age rejects the heritage of institutionalized wrongdoing. We do not accept the inevitability of evil. Like Antigone, the poetry of our age has not learned to demur in the face of disaster. Intrinsic to the intimate structure of the poem is a desire for discipline and truth that cannot allow false order.

The artist is not now, and never has been, an isolated man living in an ivory tower. Even if he sticks strictly to the periphery of public life, through his work the artist will necessarily have an impact on the lives and destinies of others. Even if an artist chooses to isolate himself in order better to work and create, by the simple fact of producing disciplined, truthful and conscientious works he will contribute to the making of a common awareness. Even if he speaks exclusively of stone and wind, the artist in his work always delivers this message to us: We are not merely animals hounded by the struggle for survival—by natural right, we are the heirs of freedom and the dignity of being.

We Portuguese writers are assembled here, united by a common language. But above all we are brought together by what Father Teilhard de Chardin called our trust in the progress of things.

Since I began by greeting those friends of mine who are present, let me end by greeting those friends who are absent, because nothing can stand between men and women who are united by one faith and one hope.

—*Sophia de Mello Breyner*

[*Art of Poetry* III was read on July 11, 1964, at a luncheon in the poet's honor held by the Sociedade Portuguesa de Escritores, which awarded her book *Livro sexto* its Grande Prémio de Poesia (Grand Prize for Poetry).]

translated by Kenneth Krabbenhoft

AFTERWORD: *A Poetry of Particular Being*

POETRY, for the Portuguese poet Sophia de Mello Breyner, means opening language to the "splendor of the presence of things." More perhaps than any other literary activity, it draws its vitality from the unmediated contemplation of that presence, paradoxically juxtaposing a fundamentally metaphysical practice with the concrete business of word-smithing. It is a craft, but a craft unlike any other because in it there is no hierarchy of master and apprentice; no difference between means and end, active skill and the product it releases into the world as both reflection of, and participant in, the awesome plurality of being. We are not surprised, then, by Sophia de Mello Breyner's explanation that the poet's *technē* "is born of the very poetry with which it is consubstantially united" (*Art of Poetry* II). The art of language is forged from this union; its motivation derives from the metaphysical link between *logos* and world that informs the sense of every word: "If a poet says 'dark,' 'wide,' 'white,' or 'stone,'" she writes, "it is because these words name a vision of the world, its connection with things" (*Art of Poetry* II). This poet's entire work reminds us that to read poetry is to achieve a heightened apprehension of the world, and that to do so requires that the reader work in partnership with the poet, tacitly dedicating himself to the task of constituting the pure presence of world in a purely present language.

A poetry which explicitly calls forth the essential identity of word and thing embodies the earliest and perhaps purest metaphysical insight of European philosophy. One must roll back the history of ideas beyond the threshold of Greek rationalism to find, with the pre-Socratics, a metaphysics which allows poetry to function as redemptive act addressing the particular being of each object in our world. Sophia de Mello Breyner's poetry breathes the freshness and astonishment felt by the first Greek thinkers who arrayed the perceived plurality of beings against the hegemony of "tò ti estí": Being as That Which Is. We are led to the pre-Socratics because in her poetry the particular essence of each thing— its *ousia*—is the touchstone of each person's apprehension of the world. For her, the legitimating being does not derive from a transcendent cause, be it Plato's Demiurge, Aristotle's Unmoved Mover or the paternal God of Judaeo-Christian tradition. Rather, it constantly affirms itself in the absolute factuality of its own existence. The poet need look no further: his task is to recognize and let flow through him this "naked entire bliss, this splendor of the presence of things" (*Art of Poetry* III). This truth has been entrusted to the poet by preference over other craftsmen because it is the legacy of the living voice, the stuff of oral tradition. It is not erudite but practical: impossible to codify, it has come down to us across the ages in the endlessly malleable emanations of the human voice—"Forms that have been passed from hand to hand down through the centuries" (*Art of Poetry* I).

The difficulty as well as the vital importance of this enterprise can be judged by the power of its opposition, for the implacable foe of the poetic reconstitution of reality is nothing less than time itself, conceived as the inexorable, ever-present distraction perpetrated by memory and anticipation, time that wrenches us away from realization of the actual in the name of shadowy hopes and fears. Sophia de Mello Breyner would purge time from the instant of perception, that "first house" of nascent sense:

> Because time pierces
> Time divides
> And time thwarts
> Tears me alive

> From the walls and floor
> Of the first house
>
> *(Muse)*

But because language is intrinsically sequential in nature, time plays a necessary role in any naming. The poet therefore adopts a frankly militant stance, perfecting her craft with "unflagging [and] intransigent obstinacy" (*Art of Poetry* II). Against time, forgetfulness, absence and loss, stands the word:

> . . . the song
> The true brother of each thing
> Incendiary of the night
> And evening's secret
>
> *(Muse)*

Its goal is the restoration of the kingdom of pure immanence in a moment of timeless perception, for "like Orpheus' body, ripped apart by the Furies, this kingdom is divided. We try to put it back together, we seek its unity, going from one thing to the next" (*Art of Poetry* I). As mere habitat, our world lies around in beautiful pieces: the task of poetry is to redeem it by bringing the parts back into presence as a whole, without ever sacrificing that complex unity of the Many to a stultifying, over-reaching One. Only the kingdom of the Many is the proper "space in which to exist."

A poet's mission is heroic because the stand against death demands a constantly reaffirmed triumph over anxiety and terror; (no wonder that the part of the human body most frequently named in this poet's work is the shoulders). The redemptive labor of language is cast as illumination, a bringing out of particular being in its sharply defined plurality from the masking ambiguity of darkness into the violent clarity of the Mediterranean sun. Like time's in-life distractions, the obfuscation that shrieks from the heart of a

misapprehended and repressive Transcendence lures us
from truth like those "strange night birds," "birds with
shrill wild cries":

> They talk to each other of night, draw
> From the abyss of slow still night
> Cruel and strident words.
> They thrust their claws into the moonlight
> And the breath of terror falls
> From their heavy wings.

(The Birds)

In this harsh climate death moves not as abstraction but as
physical sensation, a truncation of real possibilities, a mate-
rial intrusion into various ecstasies. When the poet says "I
feel the dead," she recalls not the deaths of History but
histories of the dead, from Tristan and Isolde, Orpheus and
Eurydice, the Duke of Gandia mourning Isabel of
Portugal—

> Shapes etched in the vacuum
> Of voices and gestures
>   which long ago existed

(Passing Cars)

—to an American soldier killed in Vietnam. Poetry as mor-
tal combat against the burning weight of death and grief,
patrimony of all peoples in all ages, but a political
specialty—as this Portuguese writer well knows—of our
times.

I have mentioned early Greek philosophy because
Sophia de Mello Breyner's sensibility combines the con-
crete beauty of lyrical poetry and the abstract inquiry of that
youthful metaphysics. Two thinkers are brought to mind in
this connection: the first is Heraclitus; the second, Martin
Heidegger, the twentieth-century philosopher who placed
the greatest value on that first moment in the history of the
Western mind, when the Greeks found themselves ama-

zingly in the presence of Being and for the first time gave
voice to "the actual moment of vision and surprise" ("In the
Poem"). Like the poet, Heraclitus frames the raw material
of his speculations in the simplest and most direct way:
"Whatever comes from sight, hearing, learning from expe-
rience: this I prefer."[1] When he says: "The sun is new every
day", he speaks from total immersion in the moment. This
is metaphysics, yes, but it is also poetry, because he fits the
word to the experience of particular being: this sun that I
see now, at this moment, is not the same as any other sun I
or you have ever see. And the celebrated attribution, "One
cannot step twice into the same river, nor can one grasp any
mortal substance in stable condition, but it scatters and
again gathers; it forms and dissolves, and approaches and
departs": it is this numinous, unmitigated being-present-at
the creation, each day, of the world, that speaks in the
poetry of Sophia de Mello Breyner.

Because the world presents itself here as the Many with-
out the intervening agency or mediation of a deity, the
closest the poet or philosopher can come to declaring for
authentic transcendence is by evoking the sum of dialectical
couplings—Heraclitus' "day and night, winter and sum-
mer, war and peace, satiety and hunger," individually
"named according to the pleasure of each one." He under-
stands that nature is a harsh juxtaposition of opposing
elements brought into volatile union, an interplay of thrust
and counterthrust in which "the counter-thrust brings
together, and from tones at variance comes perfect attune-
ment, and all things come to pass through conflict."

The pitiless sun of the Mediterranean lights up a similar
scene for Sophia de Mello Breyner, thing and not-thing—
the one unintelligible without the other—translated into
topical antitheses. In the visual geometry of her poems, the
angle of a window or the cupped hands of a dead soldier

both enframe and hold a representation of this world. Like-
wise, the twisted muscles and bent backs of workmen or
slaves, both indentured to the making of something that by
its very rectitude excludes their participation, be it the
ramrod posture of a stone princess or the steel-and-glass
flanks of a skyscraper. Against a background of null voice—
deserted beach, empty house, solitude inside one's skull—
there is sound: the reverberation and tumult of the streets,
the applauding sea, the breathing of night or murmur of
pinewood. Sophia de Mello Breyner's poetry is comprised
of oppositions between light and darkness (shadows along
walls, appearance of faces, distance and shine of the stars);
of odors (perfume of the linden-flower and oregano); sen-
sual experience—with the caveat that the author does not
stop at the senses but reworks them in that other category
of sensuality that is language; specifically the lush sibilants,
the long, caressing vowels and the rich nasal vibratos of
Portuguese.

For Martin Heidegger, the poet stands apart from the rest
of us because he remains always open to Being, which
"speaks itself forth" (*"spricht sich . . . aus"*) through lan-
guage.[2] Of all kinds of speaking, poetry is the purest,
Heidegger says, because it is a kind of naming that calls the
world into presence: it is "the calling that names things . . .
[that] entrusts world to the things and simultaneously
keeps the things in the splendor of the world."[3] This is the
connection that Sophia de Mello Breyner finds at the heart
of poetry: the mutual substantiation that for Heidegger
shapes man's actual everyday experience of Being as re-
vealed in particular beings. When the poet writes:

> I went and came
> And asked each thing
> Its name

> (*Coral*)

we call to mind Heidegger: "The world grants things their presence. Things bear world. World grants things." The name bares what Heidegger calls "dif-ference," that is, the division that prevails "in the between of world and thing, in their *inter*." "Dif-ference" betokens the true intimacy (not fusion) "that obtains only where the intimate—world and thing—divides itself cleanly and remains separated." The consistency of Sophia de Mello Breyner's poetry, which affirms magnificently the plurality of world, derives from her attention to this "dif-ference."

Naming saves things, the world, from namelessness, that is, nonexistence in the mind of man, death, but only in the eternal present. For this reason mere longing for the past in the form of nostalgia, or the wistful contemplation of time's evanescence (something like the quintessentially Portuguese sentiment called *"saudade"*) find no place in Sophia de Mello Breyner's redemptive poetics, which is rigorously located in the excruciating and ecstatic intensity of the present. Naming's work is:

> To bring the picture the wall the wind
> The flower the glass the shine on wood
> And the cold chaste clearness of water
> To the clean severe world of the poem
>
> To save from death decay and ruin
> The actual moment of vision and surprise
> And keep in the real world
> The real gesture of a hand touching the table.
>
> (*In the Poem*)

She takes note of the fact because the landscape that fills her eye was once itself crowded with gods, but she knows full well and accepts that the gods are dead because we have killed them. There is therefore no yearning for either epic or tragic heroism. There are ghosts in her poetry, but they state Heideggerian "dif-ference," not regret. There may be a note of admiration as well, but the same admiration attaches itself to the inanimate realm(s) of particular being—"the kingdom we search for on the green sea's beaches, in the suspended blue of the night, in the purity of whitewash, in a polished pebble, in the scent of oregano" (*Art of Poetry* I). The sense-impressions here belong not exclusively to Greece but to non-Mediterranean Portugal, too: tangy perfume of juniper in the hot sea breeze at Estoril; dusty pines on a cool hillside by the Mondego; somber mustard-yellow gorse at Cabo São Vicente.

There is a discrete sensuality in Sophia de Mello Breyner's poetry: the wind caresses, the hills embrace. Her colors are often soft seagreen, skyblue, merciful glow of evening gold. Yet underlying it is an ascetic devotion, a withdrawal unlike the mystic's in that it moves toward the world rather than away from it:

> Don't touch anything, don't look, don't recollect
> One step enough
> To shatter the furniture baked
> By endless, unused days of sunlight.
>
> Don't remember, don't anticipate.
> You do not share the nature of a fruit:
> Nothing here that time or sun will ripen.
>
> (*Listen*)

The enemy, the constant threat, is the inability to say:

> When words batter the walls
> In blind, wild swoops of trapped birds
> And the horror of being winged
> Shrills like a clock in the vacuum.
>
> (*Sibyls*)

The *Dasein* (Being) to which she directs her imprecations in moments of despair is therefore identifiable as the bespeaking of utter presence, puzzling only when it is withheld from our attention:

> I beg You to manifest
> Ask You to flood everything.
> Your kingdom to anticipate
> And inundate the earth
> In rash, ferocious Spring.
>
> *(I Call You)*

We know that the manifestation will be universal, apportioned amidst all things according to their unique selves, given as "the richness of every presence" (*Never Again*).

Because what is given and received is for Sophia de Mello Breyner literally all or nothing, poetry demands obstinacy and perseverance; hence a prerequisite individualism, the refusal to accept the known, the struggle against the *doxa* ("received opinion") within the *doxa*. There is terrible irony in her infrequent subscription to *doxa*, as when she confesses that her gods, like everyone else's, are more dead than the stonebound friezes at Pergamon:

> Also in the twilight where I live
> The gods are defeated
>
> *(Torso)*

These moments are few: she recoils from tropes that distance writer from writing because her poetry is intensely committed to the world in a moral as well as a metaphysical sense. She would abhor the falsity of the distinction, since "He who sees the shocking splendor of the world is logically led to see the shocking misery of the world" (*Art of Poetry* III). Even if the poet chooses to work in solitude, she says, "even if he speaks exclusively of stones and wind, the artist in his work always delivers this message to us: We are not merely animals hounded by the struggle for survival—by natural law we are the heirs of freedom and the dignity of being" (*Art of Poetry* III). And: "the fight for justice is a basic aspect of all poetic works . . . because justice is inseparable from the balance of things, the order of the world with which the poet wants to integrate his song" (*Art of Poetry* III)—the Heraclitean balance of health and sickness, justice and injustice, freedom and oppression, splendor and suffering. Tempered by the condition of being Portuguese in mid-twentieth century, Sophia de Mello Breyner writes:

> This is the night
> Thick with jackals
> Weighted with grief
>
> (*This Is the Time*)

Classical in its visual vocabulary, evocation of myth, physical landscape; modern in its godlessness, its radical anthropocentrism, and the ensuing charge to the poet-metaphysician: constitute the world in the order of your craft so as to prevent it from degenerating into the inchoate dispersion of death. Sophia de Mello Breyner's poetry teaches that the redemption of the world is man's work, and poetry is his tool. There is no God, and the gods have been vanquished because they proved susceptible to discursive reason. When Sophia de Mello Breyner reminds us that the meditation on destruction pledges us to a higher allegiance, she is referring of course to life, but not life as hegemonous whole: life as constant awareness of the constellated aggregate of existents. Life lived now, because the past gives no guarantee of the present, and the present cannot assure the future. Her poetry breathes with the sharp insight of the instant, the moment when mind turns to calling and bringing the world into proximity.

Heraclitus wrote that man's character is his "*daimon*," or destiny. Like character, the poet's language also bears the imprint of his "*daimon*." In the case of a metaphysical poet like Sophia de Mello Breyner, the chronological schemata of literary history, based on movements and generations, can be an inadequate descriptive tool. Other poets of the Mediterranean come to mind, like Valéry and Elytis, and there are of course similarities between her work and that of other Portuguese-language poets like her compatriot Jorge de Sena or her Brazilian friend João Cabral de Melo Neto. The shadow of Fernando Pessoa, the greatest Portuguese poet since Camões, inevitably falls across the contemporary scene, and Sophia de Mello Breyner does indeed evoke him in one of her longest poems. For her he was above all the poet of exile and absence:

> And you had many faces
> So that being no one you could say everything
> You travelled the reverse the inverse the adverse
> (*Cyclades*)

But this invocation is one craftsman's homage to another very different sort of writer, since what stands out in a comparison of the two is the self-assured homogeneity of her voice, whereas Pessoa made a craft of being ill at ease with a single poetic voice. This quality of Sophia de Mello Breyner has been remarked by critics: the rare consistency of her verse from her first published works to her most recent. The explanation is simple, if you will, and can be put as a query: why do so many poets so often change their voice, when the world of particular being does not change at all? To this poet's perceiving eye, fixed on the underlying, balanced unity of opposites, there is only one vision of the endlessly meaningful Presence of all things, the many whose plurality is the meaning we search for.

—*Kenneth Krabbenhoft*
New York University

NOTES

1. The translations of Heraclitus are from Charles H. Kahn, editor and translator, *The Art and Thought of Heraclitus* (Cambridge: Cambridge University Press, 1983).

2. Martin Heidegger, *Being and Time*, translated by John Macquarrie and Edward Robinson (New York: Harper and Row, 1962).

3. Martin Heidegger, *Poetry, Language, Thought*, translated by Albert Hofstadter (New York: Harper and Row, 1975).

DATE DUE

GAYLORD No. 2333 | | | PRINTED IN U.S.A.